FIGHTING FORCES ON THE SEA

Cruisers

LYNN M. STONE

Rourke
Publishing LLC
Vero Beach, Florida 32964

© 2006 Rourke Publishing LLC

All rights reserved. No part of this book may be reproduced or utilized in any form or by any means, electronic or mechanical including photocopying, recording, or by any information storage and retrieval system without permission in writing from the publisher.

www.rourkepublishing.com

PHOTO CREDITS: p. 5, 6, 9, 10, 12, 13, 15, 16, 18, 19, 29 courtesy U.S. Navy title page, p. 20, 21, 22, 24, 26 courtesy Naval Institute p. 23, 27 courtesy U.S. Department of Defense National Archives

Title page: *USS* Alaska, *one of three "big cruisers" built for the U.S. Navy in the early 1940s, was much bigger than today's guided missile cruisers.*

Editor: Frank Sloan

Library of Congress Cataloging-in-Publication Data

Stone, Lynn M.
  Cruisers / Lynn M. Stone.
      p. cm. -- (Fighting forces on the sea)
  Includes bibliographical references and index.
  ISBN 1-59515-463-9 (hardcover)
 1. Cruisers (Warships)--Juvenile literature. I. Title. II. Series.

V820.S76 2006
623.825'3--dc22

2005014844

Printed in the USA

CG/CG

www.rourkepublishing.com – sales@rourkepublishing.com
Post Office Box 3328, Vero Beach, FL 32964

1-800-394-7055

Table of Contents

CHAPTER 1 Cruisers 4

CHAPTER 2 Cruiser Characteristics 10

CHAPTER 3 Early History 20

CHAPTER 4 World War II 22

CHAPTER 5 After World War II 26

CHAPTER 6 The Future of Cruisers 28

Glossary 30

Index 32

Further Reading/Websites to Visit 32

CRUISERS

CHAPTER ONE

Modern U.S. Navy guided missile cruisers are large, multi-mission warships bristling with modern weapons, including cruise missiles. With their range of weapons and highly advanced radar and weapons systems, guided missile cruisers have the capability to attack more than one target at once. The target may be on land, in the sea, or in the air. These high-tech weapons help make guided missile cruisers (designated CG by the Navy) among the world's most powerful warships.

▲ *USS* Philippine Sea *is one of the U.S. Navy's multi-mission guided missile cruisers.*

▲
The guided missile cruiser Lake Erie *lies at her berth in Pearl Harbor, Hawaii.*

Each of the Navy's remaining 22 guided missile cruisers is part of the *Ticonderoga* **class**. The first ship in an original class of 27, the USS *Ticonderoga* was **commissioned** in January, 1983. The final ship in the class, USS *Port Royal*, was commissioned in 1994. Five of the *Ticonderoga*-class cruisers were **decommissioned** in the early 2000s.

Guided missile cruisers are primarily used as part of a Navy carrier battle group. Battle groups consist of several warships. Typically, these ships work to support and protect one or more aircraft carriers. Cruisers and their cousins—guided missile **destroyers**—are designed to ward off enemy submarines, surface ships, and aircraft. Beyond their carrier escort duties, guided missile cruisers can support **amphibious** forces, or they can operate alone.

The *Ticonderoga*-class ships were designed in the 1970s as destroyers, not cruisers. *Ticonderogas* were built on the **hulls** and **propulsion** systems of the *Spruance*-class destroyers (DDG). But as the building program advanced, the ship originally foreseen changed. The new Aegis Combat System and other installations added weight, hiking the ships' **displacement**—the weight of water a ship displaces—by almost 1,000 tons (910 metric tons). Cruisers traditionally have been larger than destroyers, so the increase in weight prompted the Navy in 1980 to rename the new class of ships cruisers.

FACT FILE ★

THE BIGGEST AMERICAN CRUISERS IN WORLD WAR II HAD A DISPLACEMENT OF 27,500 TONS (25,425 METRIC TONS) AND WERE MUCH LARGER THAN TODAY'S GUIDED-MISSILE CRUISERS.

Cruisers of the early and mid-20th century were considerably bigger than destroyers, but somewhat smaller, faster, and armed with less firepower than battleships.

▲
Normally used as part of the U.S. Navy's various battle groups of ships, the guided missile cruiser USS Lake Erie *leads the parade on the way to the Arabian Gulf.*

Cruiser Characteristics

Ticonderoga-class cruisers have a crew of 364, including 20 officers. They guide a formidable ship that's 567 feet (173 meters) long—more than one and one-half times the length of a football field—and can knife through the sea at more than 30 knots (34.5 miles, 55 kilometers) per hour.

▲
Although built on Spruance-*class destroyer hulls, the guided missile cruisers, like* Gettysburg *here, are heavier ships than destroyers.*

Cruiser Specifications

Ticonderoga class - CG

Powerplant:
4 gas turbine engines, 2 shafts; 80,000 shaft horsepower

Length:
567 feet (173 meters)

Beam:
55 feet (17 meters)

Displacement:
9,600 tons (8,376 metric tons) fully loaded

Speed:
30+ knots (34.5 miles, 55 kilometers per hour)

Aircraft:
2 SH-60 Seahawk (LAMPS III equipped) helicopters

Ship's company:
24 officers, 340 enlisted

Armament:
Standard missiles, ASROC (VLA) missiles, Tomahawk cruise missiles; MK-46 torpedoes; 2 MK 45 5-inch (13-centimeter)/54 caliber lightweight guns; 2 Phalanx Close-In Weapons Systems

Commissioning date, first ship:
1983

▲
Part of an aircraft carrier strike group, the Vincennes *knifes through the western Pacific Ocean.*

The computer-based Aegis Combat System is the heart of a guided missile cruiser's capability for both defense and attack. The Aegis system finds targets, tracks them, and sends the commands for their destruction.

The core of the system is highly sophisticated phased-array radar, known as the AN/SPY-1. It can perform search, track, and missile guidance functions of over 100 targets at the same time!

Another important part of the *Ticonderoga* class is its Vertical Launching System (VLS). VLS permits ships greater missile selection, adding to their **survivability** and their firepower.

▲
Aboard the USS Lake Champlain, an operations specialist monitors air radar contacts in the ship's Combat Information Center.

Most of a guided missile cruiser's weaponry is in its missiles. The ship's surface-to-air missile is a medium-range weapon, the Standard missile. Its main job is to protect ships in the battle force from aircraft. The *Ticonderogas'* VLA missile is a three-stage, anti-submarine rocket that delivers a torpedo.

FACT FILE

Spruance destroyers and *Ticonderoga* cruisers are similar in appearance and even in weaponry. The most recent guided missile destroyers, of the *Arleigh Burke* class, displace nearly as much water (9,200 tons; 8,372 metric tons) as *Ticonderoga* cruisers (9,600 tons; 8,736 metric tons).

▲
A Standard missile (SM-3) blasts from the vertical launch system of an Aegis guided missile cruiser.

▲
The guided missile cruiser USS Anzio *launches a Tomahawk land attack missile in support of Operation Iraqi Freedom in 2003.*

For attacks on land targets, *Ticonderoga*-class ships are armed with Tomahawk cruise missiles. These extremely accurate, long-range missiles, which weigh up to 3,500 pounds (1,588 kilograms), fly long distances at extremely low altitudes. Tomahawks can fly from 700 to 1,350 miles (1,126 to 2,173 kilometers) at speeds of about 550 miles (885 kilometers) per hour. One version of the Tomahawk contains the devastating W80 **nuclear** warhead. The latest generation Tomahawks can be reprogrammed while in flight to strike pre-programmed targets.

FACT FILE

WITH ONE EXCEPTION (USS *THOMAS S. GATES*), EACH OF THE NAVY'S 22 GUIDED-MISSILE CRUISERS IS NAMED AFTER A FAMOUS BATTLE, RANGING FROM THE REVOLUTIONARY WAR (USS *BUNKER HILL*) THROUGH THE CIVIL WAR (USS *ANTIETAM*), WORLD WAR II (USS *NORMANDY*), AND KOREA (USS *CHOSIN*).

▲
Another of a guided missile cruiser's weapons is the .54 caliber MK-45, 5-inch (13-centimeter) lightweight gun, being fired here from the deck of the USS Leyte Gulf.

In addition to missiles, guided missile cruisers have the Phalanx Close-In Weapons System (CIWS) and its 20-millimeter guns. The system detects, tracks, and locks onto targets, such as incoming anti-ship missiles, aircraft, small, high-speed boats, and even surface mines.

A *Ticonderoga*-class ship also has aboard two, twin-engine SH-60 Seahawk helicopters equipped with high-tech undersea weapons systems and submarine detection electronics. While an airborne Seahawk patrols the ocean away from the cruiser, its communications system process data and relay it to the control room of the ship.

▲
A pair of Seahawk helicopters participates in an air power demonstration along with the guided missile cruiser USS Vella Gulf.

Early history

In the 1880s the U.S. Navy began commissioning its first steel-built, steam-powered cruisers. Prior to that, warships had been largely fashioned from wood and powered by sail.

In the next 20 years, the U.S. cruiser force was involved in the Spanish-American War (1898) and in several smaller conflicts in Chile, Hawaii, Korea, Cuba, the Dominican Republic, Morocco, and present-day Lebanon.

◀ *Francis Muller's painting shows the USS* Olympia, *a steam-powered, steel cruiser launched in 1892. The* Olympia *fought in the Spanish-American War and again during World War I.*

▲
The USS San Diego, *the U.S. Navy's armored cruiser no. 6, became the only large American warship lost in World War I when it hit a German mine near Fire Island, New York.*

When the United States joined France and England against Germany in World War I (1914-1918) in 1917, 24 American cruisers helped ship nearly 1 million soldiers of the American Expeditionary Force to Europe—without loss of a single life to enemy naval action.

World War II

By the start of World War II (1939-1945), the Navy had ordered *Atlanta*-class cruisers with dual-purpose weapons: antiaircraft guns as well as the customary big deck guns. In 1940, the Navy ordered the first of 27 improved *Cleveland*-class cruisers.

▲
The light cruiser Atlanta, *shown here in late 1941, sank in late 1942 after taking heavy damage from Japanese ships and planes and accidentally from an American destroyer during the naval Battle of Guadalcanal.*

▲
Gun crews of an American cruiser cover an amphibious landing on Mindoro, in the Philippines, in December, 1944.

After America's entry into the war in December, 1941, U.S. cruisers—both heavy and light types—were often used to protect aircraft carriers against ships and planes and to bombard shore targets. Cruisers were the biggest American warships to be in frequent naval battles with Japanese ships.

▲
The cruiser Indianapolis *was photographed on July 10, 1945, after being repaired from battle damage and shortly before she sank.*

While American cruisers handed out punishment, they also took it. The United States lost seven heavy cruisers and three light cruisers during the war, four of them at the Battle of Savo Island in 1942.

The last American cruiser sunk was the USS *Indianapolis*, torpedoed by a Japanese submarine on July 29, 1945. Traveling alone, the *Indianapolis* sank in just 12 minutes. Distress calls from the *Indianapolis* went unheard. The Navy did not know the *Indianapolis* had disappeared until August 2, when a patrol plane spotted life rafts. Nearly 900 crewmen died in the disaster, although 317 were rescued.

FACT FILE

NAVY CRUISERS HAVE HAD MANY NAMES OVER THE YEARS. ITS SCOUT CRUISERS OF THE EARLY 1900S WERE RENAMED "LIGHT CRUISERS." THE NAVY HAD SIX "BATTLE CRUISERS" FROM 1916 TO 1922. NAVY "GUNBOATS" OF 1920 WERE RENAMED "PROTECTED CRUISERS," THEN "LIGHT CRUISERS." SOME OF THE LIGHT CRUISERS OF THE EARLY 1930S WERE RENAMED "HEAVY CRUISERS." THE SIX SHIPS OF THE LARGE CRUISER CLASS OF 1940 WERE SO MUCH BIGGER THAN THE HEAVY CRUISERS OF THE TIME THAT THEY SIMPLY BECAME "BIG CRUISERS."

After World War II

CHAPTER FIVE

During the Korean War (1950-1953), American cruisers shelled North Korean shore targets. Cruisers helped cover both the landing and removal of troops at battle sites. Cruisers operated as support ships off the coast of Vietnam in the late 1960s and 1970s.

▲
The light cruiser USS Bremerton *was one of the American warships sent to Korea to shell enemy positions during the Korean War.*

The long Cold War (1945-1991) between the Soviet Union and the United States prompted continuing improvements in American naval forces. Several World War II-era cruisers were fitted with new electronics and missiles. The USS *Long Beach*, commissioned in 1961, became the world's first nuclear-powered surface warship. (None of America's cruisers is presently nuclear-powered.)

After the Cold War, the United States downsized the Navy in numbers of ships. The big cruisers are gone, replaced by the much smaller, but more **lethal**, guided missile cruisers.

▲
The guided missile cruiser Canberra's *guns open up on a target in Vietnam in March, 1967.*

The Future of Cruisers

Chapter Six

All guided missile cruisers are scheduled for modernization, beginning in 2006. Systems upgrades will improve the ships' war-fighting capability, including a place for a **ballistic** missile defense platform. And over the horizon lies the CG(X), the next generation of cruiser. The emphasis will be on a ship that is **stealthier**—more difficult to detect by radar—and has more power while, at the same time, uses a smaller crew. The Navy, after all, has to watch its budgets as well as its "boats."

▲
USS Vicksburg, *sailing under an Arabian Gulf sunrise, will be among the guided missile cruisers scheduled for a modernization program that begins in 2006.*

Glossary

amphibious (am FIB ee us) — of land and water, such as Marines landing by sea to fight on land

ballistic (bul LIS tik) — referring to certain long-range missiles that climb in a high arc under self propulsion and then fall freely

class (KLAS) — a group of ships manufactured to the same, or very similar, specifications, such as the *Ticonderoga* class of American cruisers

commissioned (kuh MISH und) — to have been placed into official service by the U.S. Navy

decommissioned (DEE kuh MISH und) — when a ship has been taken out of active service by the U.S. Navy

destroyers (duh STROI urz) — surface warships traditionally used to defend larger, slower ships from submarines (modern destroyers are armed with guided missiles for multi-missions)

displacement (dis PLAY smunt) — the water displaced by a floating ship; the tonnage of the water displaced

hulls (HULZ) — the main frame and bodies of ships

lethal (LEE thul) — deadly

nuclear (NYU klee ur) — providing atomic energy in a controlled, powerful way

propulsion (pruh PUL shun) — the system by which a ship moves under its own power, such as steam power that is coupled with propeller blades

stealthier (STELTH ee ur) — more difficult to detect by radar

survivability (sur VYE vuh BIL uh tee) — the ability to survive; in the case of a ship, to stay afloat and operational

INDEX

Aegis Combat System 8, 12
aircraft carriers 23
Atlanta class 22
battle group 7
Battle of Savo Island 25
battleships 9
Cleveland class 22
Cold War 27
destroyers 7, 8
helicopters 7, 8
Korean War 26
missiles 4, 14, 17, 18, 27
radar 13
Spanish-American War 20
Ticonderoga class 7, 8, 10, 11, 13, 17, 19
USS *Indianapolis* 25
Vertical Launching System 13
weapons 4, 14
World War I 21
World War II 22-25

FURTHER READING

Green, Michael. *Cruisers*. Capstone, 1997

Nelson, Peter. *Left for Dead: A Young Man's Search for Justice for the USS Indianapolis*. Bantam Doubleday Dell Books for Young Readers, 2002

WEBSITES TO VISIT

http://www.chinfo.navy.mil/navpalib/ships/cruisers/
http://www.chinfo.navy.mil/navpalib/factfile/ships/ship-cru.html

ABOUT THE AUTHOR

Lynn M. Stone is the author and photographer of many children's books. Lynn is a former teacher who travels worldwide to pursue his varied interests.